The Resurrection
in the Great Story of
JESUS

Stephen Joseph Wolf

idjc.org

The Resurrection in the Great Story of Jesus
Copyright © 2023 Stephen Joseph Wolf
All rights reserved. No part of this book may be copied or reproduced in any form or by any means, except for the inclusion of brief quotations in a review, without the written permission of the author or publisher.

Scripture in the Comparative Texts, rendered as a study aid in the present tense, and the cover art are by Stephen Joseph Wolf.

published by IDJC press; printed and distributed by Ingram

ISBN: 978-1-937081-78-2

Stephen Joseph Wolf is retired, a former parish priest (22 lents & holy weeks), spiritual director and retreat leader, and former certified public accountant (14 tax seasons), and before that worked as a landscaper, desk clerk, laundry worker, janitor, paper boy, and student, growing up the second of eight sons of a parish secretary and Nashville's best television repairman. He completed a B.S. at MTSU, an M.B.A. at Belmont University, and an M.Div. at Mundelein Seminary.

He continues to write poems and songs and paints folk art icons, sings baritone for the LGBTQ+ chorus *Nashville in Harmony*, plays the ukulele with *Music for Seniors* and others, volunteers as bookkeeper for two non-profits, serves on the board of *PFLAG Nashville*, gathers with the LGBTQ+Catholic group *Always God's Children*, and lives in Nashville with his husband Billy.

Six-Chapter Works for Faith Sharing by Stephen Joseph Wolf

PONDERING OUR FAITH: with the new creed
TREE OF LIFE: Saint Bonaventure on the Christ Story
GOD'S ONES: a *so-what* book for the baptized
FORTY PENANCES FOR SPIRITUAL EXERCISE
GOD'S MONEY: where faith meets life in the world
BEING SPOUSES: from celibate observation
TWELVE-STEP SPIRITUALITY FOR CHRISTIANS
ANGER THE JESUS WAY
PLANNING MY OWN FUNERAL? (four chapters)
THE PASSION IN THE GREAT STORY OF JESUS
THE RESURRECTION IN THE GREAT STORY OF JESUS

www.idjc.org

The RESURRECTION in the GREAT STORY of JESUS

A Group Process		4
Possible Group Ground Rules		5
People of the Resurrection		6
Most Scholars (not all)…		7
Week 1	**THE EMPTY TOMB**	8
	Song: *Jesus Christ Is Ris'n Today*	
Week 2	**MARY MAGDALENE**	20
	Song: *Ye Sons & Daughters of the King*	
Week 3	**THE ROAD TO EMMAUS**	30
	Song: *I Know That My Redeemer Lives*	
Week 4	**THE UPPER ROOM**	40
	Song: *That Night th'Apostles Met in Fear*	
Week 5	**SEASHORE BREAKFAST**	50
	Song: *Let Us Break Bread Together*	
Week 6	**THE GREAT COMMISSION & THE ASCENSION**	60
	Song: *In Christ There Is No East or West*	
Additional titles by the author		72

A GROUP PROCESS

This is the simple process for a 90 minute group meeting:

1. A song that most people know.
2. Some word of God from the Bible.
3. Some narrative on the Scripture or theme.
4. Some questions to prompt discussion.
5. A closing prayer to end on time.

Faith sharing with *The Resurrection in the Great Story of Jesus* will be a bit different from other group processes. The focus is on the text, taking as given that the editing done for each of the four gospels was deliberate. Each gospel, written for a specific community, is God's inspired word for all peoples and decades. We engage these four accounts in the tradition of the Church, and listen for what grabs us and intersects the culture and our own life experience.

For more guidance on leading a group, visit *www.idjc.org*. Some will want to read this book on their own, and that is normally fine. On this one, gather a handful of friends and read it together. Blessings!

Steve Wolf

POSSIBLE GROUP GROUND RULES
Faith Sharing is:

Regular: I will do my best to make all sessions.

Discerned: There is no need to answer every question. Questions are offered to prompt sharing of stories; it is acceptable to simply offer an observation.

Voluntary: No one is required to share. The tone is invitational; verbal participation is encouraged but not demanded.

Not Interrupted: When someone is sharing, everyone listens before commenting or speaking. Side conversations are avoided, one person at a time.

Not Contradicted: The sharing is based on the person's own life story, so conclusions or critiques of what is shared are not appropriate. Avoid trying to take away feelings with comments like, *You shouldn't feel that way.*

Done in "I" Language: beginning with *I think* or *I feel* rather than *Mary said* or *Joe thinks*.

Confidential: What is said in the group stays in the group.

_{These ground rules are drawn from Joye Gros' *Theological Reflections*, Loyola Press, 2002. Groups are free to alter them as they wish.}

I agree with the group ground rules. (Signature and Date)

PEOPLE of the RESURRECTION

Mary the Magdalene - apostle to the apostles
Other Mary - in Matthew, mother of James & Joseph
Mary the mother of James - in Luke
Salome - in Mark
Joanna - in Luke 8:3, wife of Herod's steward Chuza
Other Women from Galilee - in Luke
Angel of the Lord - in Matthew, rolls stone away
Young Human - in Mark, in a white robe
Two Humans - in Luke, in shining clothing
Two Angels - in John, in white
Peter - Simon Peter in John, not named in Matthew
Beloved Disciple - traditionally John of Zebedee
Jesus - by name, in Luke also called the Nazarene
Those Who Had Been with Him - for the 3 years
Some of the Guards - in Matthew, bribed to tell a lie
Chief Priests & Presbyters - Sanhedrin members
Two Disciples Walking - simple story in Mark
Cleopas & Companion - detailed story in Luke
The Rest - in Luke, with the Eleven hear the women
The Eleven - the Twelve minus Judas Iscariat
Thomas - called Twin, one of the original Twelve
Nathanael - in John, one of the seven at Galilee
Sons of Zebedee - James & John, two of the Twelve
Two Other Disciples - in John, at Galilee breakfast
All Nations - in Matthew, where disciples are sent

```
                        MARK
                   (written about)
other Matthew        75 A.D.?         other Lukan
   material          ↙      ↘           material
      ↓                                    ↓
  MATTHEW                                LUKE
(written about)                      (written about)
   85 A.D.?)    ↖              ↗        85 A.D.?)
                 Sayings of Jesus (?)
                       (lost?)
```

Most scholars (not all) hold that the Gospel of Mark was written before the others. If we date the passion and resurrection at about 33 A.D. and the editing of what we now call the Gospel of Mark at about 75 A.D., that leaves us with about 40 years of the faithful carrying these narratives in oral traditions.

An early collection of sayings of Jesus (long ago lost if it did exist), called "Q" after the German word for "source," was likely used by the editors of Matthew and Luke, the best theory being that the editors of Matthew and Luke each had in front of them the Gospel of Mark, the "Q" Sayings of Jesus, plus their own unique traditions and teachings about Jesus.

The consensus of the scholars is that John developed from its own tradition, independent of the others, perhaps around 90 A.D.(?).

1

THE EMPTY TOMB

Leader   Try to notice as we proceed today if a **seed** is planted, a **memory** is provoked, a **question** is raised, or an **action** is prompted.

So let us sing together as we are able:

All   **Je-sus Christ is ris'n to-day**\,
Our/ tri\-umph-ant/ ho-ly day,
Who did once up-on the cross\,
Suf/-fer\ to re/-deem our loss,
Hymns of praise, then, let us sing,
Un/-to\ Christ, our/ heav'n-ly King,
Who/ en\-dured the cross and grave\,
Sin\-ners\ to/ re/-deem and save.

But the pain which he en-dured\,
Our/ sal\-va-tion/ has pro-cured,
Now a-bove the sky he's King\,
Where/ the\ an-gels/ ev-er sing,
Sing we to our God a-bove,
Praise/ e\-ter-nal/ as God's love,
Praise/ God\, all you heav'n-ly host\,
Fa\-ther\, Son/, and/ Ho-ly Ghost.

Text: Bohemian Carol, *Surrexit Christus hodie*, 1372, tr. by John Walsh, 1708, stanzas 1 & 2a by John Arnold, 1749; 2b by Charles Wesley, 1740, altered
Music: 77 77 EASTER HYMN without alleluias, *Lyra Davidica*, 1708

THE RESURRECTION IN THE GREAT STORY OF JESUS

Leader   1st Corinthians 15:1-8

A reading from the First Letter
of Saint Paul to the Corinthians:

Now I am reminding you, brothers and sisters, of the gospel I preached to you, which you indeed received and in which you also stand. Through it you are also being saved, if you hold fast to the word I preached to you, unless you believed in vain. For I handed on to you as of first importance what I also received: *that* Christ died for our sins in accordance with the scriptures; *that* he was buried; *that* he was raised on the third day in accordance with the scriptures; *that* he appeared to Cephas, then to the Twelve. After that, he appeared to more than five hundred brothers and sisters at once, most of whom are still living, though some have fallen asleep. After that he appeared to James, then to all the apostles. Last of all, as to one born abnormally, he appeared to me.

     The word of the Lord.
All   **Thanks be to God.**

Leader Let us take five silent minutes with the story of the empty tomb on the next two pages.

MATTHEW	MARK
28:1-8 Easter Vigil A	16:1-8 Easter Vigil B

1 After the sabbath, the first day of the week dawning, Mary the Magdalene and the other Mary come to view the grave. 2 Behold <u>a mega earthquake</u> occurs, for an <u>angel</u> of the Lord descends out of heaven and approaching rolls away <u>the stone</u> and <u>sits upon it</u>, 3 appearing as lightning and with clothes white as snow. 4 The <u>guards</u>, shaken from fear, become <u>as dead</u>. 5 The angel says to the women, "<u>Be not afraid</u>; for I know that you seek Jesus, the one crucified. 6 He is not here, for <u>he is risen</u> as he said. <u>Come and see</u> the place where he lay. 7 <u>Go</u> quickly and <u>tell</u> his disciples that he is risen from the dead, and behold he goes before you to Galilee. There you will see him. Behold, I have told you." 8 Going away from the tomb quickly, with <u>fear and great joy</u>, they run to tell his disciples.	1 When the sabbath has passed Mary the Magdalene, and Mary the mother of James, and Salome <u>buy spices</u> that they might come and anoint him. 2 Very early on the first day of the week, they come upon the tomb at the <u>rising of the sun</u>. 3 They ask themselves, "Who will roll away the <u>stone</u> out of the door of the tomb for us?" 4 <u>Looking up</u> they behold that the stone has been rolled back, for it is <u>mega large</u>. 5 Entering into the tomb, they see a <u>young human</u> sitting on the right clothed in a <u>white robe</u>, and they are <u>utterly amazed</u>. 6 He says to them: "<u>Be not amazed</u>. Jesus you seek, the Nazarene who was crucified; <u>he is risen</u>. He is not here. Behold the place where they laid him. 7 But you <u>go tell</u> his disciples and Peter that he goes before you to Galilee; there you will see him, as he told you." 8 Going forth <u>they flee</u> from the tomb; trembling and bewilderment have them, and <u>they tell no one anything</u>, for they are afraid.

THE EMPTY TOMB

LUKE
24:1-12 Easter Vigil C

1 On day one of the week, while still very early, <u>they</u> come upon the tomb carrying <u>spices</u> which they have prepared. 2 They find <u>the stone</u> rolled away from the tomb, and entering they do not find the body of the Lord Jesus. 4 As they are <u>perplexed</u> about this, behold, <u>two humans stand</u> by them in <u>shining clothing</u>. 5 Becoming <u>terrified</u> and bending their faces to the earth, they say to them, "Why do you seek the living one among the dead?
6 He is not here, but <u>is risen</u>. Remember how he spoke to you while yet in Galilee, saying,
7 'It is <u>fitting</u> that the Son of humanity be delivered into the hands of sinful humans and be crucified, and on the third day to rise again.'"
8 They remember his words, and 9 returning from the tomb tell all these things to the Eleven and to all the rest. 10 They are Mary the Magdalene and Joanna and Mary the mother of James, and the rest with them who tell these things to the apostles.
11 These words seem to them as folly, and <u>they do not believe them</u>. 12 But Peter rises, runs to the tomb, bending over looks in and sees the linen clothes by themselves, and goes home amazed at what has happened.

JOHN
20:1-9 Easter Sunday ABC

1 Now on day one of the week, Mary the Magdalene comes in the early darkness to the tomb, and sees <u>the stone</u> having been taken away from the tomb. 2 So <u>she runs</u> and comes to Simon Peter and the other disciple Jesus loves, and says to them, "They took the Lord out of the tomb, and <u>we do not know where they put him</u>." 3 Peter and the other disciple go forth and come to the tomb. 4 The two run together, but the other disciple runs before Peter more quickly and comes first to the tomb, 5 and bending sees the linens lying, but does not enter. 6 Simon Peter also comes following, and enters the tomb, and sees <u>the linens</u> lying, 7 and <u>the cloth</u> which had been on his head, not lying with the linens, but apart in one place, having been <u>rolled up</u>. 8 <u>The other disciple</u> also enters, having come first to the tomb, and he <u>sees and believes</u>, 9 for they did not yet understand the scripture, that he felt it <u>fitting</u> to rise again from the dead.

after five minutes of silence

Leader Our process is simple. We will take turns reading one paragraph at a time.
If reading in public is not your thing, just say "pass, please."

All of this happens on the first day of the week, sometimes called the eighth day of the seven-day week, so a new beginning. After marking a full day of Jesus being dead on Holy Saturday, a Sabbath, a day of rest, God is at work again.

Remember that most Christians do what we do on Sunday instead of Saturday because Easter happened on a Sunday.

In ministry, the only calendar that made sense to me was one that showed the week as Monday leading to Sunday, for all the week built up to the busy day of the Sunday celebration of the Resurrection. In those days that would always include a donut; in these days it is ice cream on Sunday night.

I may be the last human to use a paper calendar; does your calendar have a first day of the week? What effect does that have on how you mark the days of your life?

MATTHEW

Mary Magdalene and another Mary know where the tomb is because they had sat there on Friday watching Jesus be buried. We are told this *other Mary* is the mother of James and Joseph (see Mt 27:56), who are named as brothers to Jesus (see Mt 13:55). Is she then an aunt to Jesus? More on Mary Magdalene in the next chapter.

The *mega earthquake* reminds us of the earlier earthquake at the death of Jesus. In my weird sense of humor, it makes me think of the scene in the movie *It's a Wonderful Life* when thunder signals that George Bailey's wish of never having been born is granted, and the angel Clarence shouts out the door, "well you don't have to make all *that* fuss about it!"

As a kind of porter or doorkeeper to the empty tomb Matthew gives us one angel, Mark gives us one young human in a white robe, and Luke two humans in shining clothing not as porters but waiting in the tomb. John makes no mention of a doorkeeper.

The angel *works* to roll the stone for the sabbath is over, and then sits on it, like the original *sabbath* rest after the work of creation, gazing on the work that has been done.

The angel action of rolling the stone and sitting on it lets the women and the guards give witness that no one has moved the body, though the guards would be later bribed to say otherwise, and this is suspected in John.

The angel's invitation *Come and See* were spoken by Jesus to two early seekers (John 1:39).

The guards have a fear that shakes them into a deadness, while the Mary's have a fear that is joined with great joy.

What do you make of this, that Peter is not named in Matthew's resurrection story but is lumped in with the remaining Eleven? Indeed, when Peter is last mentioned by name in this gospel he is weeping, after the cock crows when he denies Jesus for the third time.

MARK

Three women bring spices, and we are not told how the mega stone has been moved.

The phrase *rising of the sun* works phonetically as a play on the words *rising of the son*. Does this work in other languages?

Young human is the same description of the one who ran away naked from the arrest scene. Some think he is the author of this gospel.

In the gospel miracle stories, Jesus often tells people to not tell anyone about him; they tell anyway. Here the *young human* gives the Mary's and Salome a message for the disciples, but they are afraid and bewildered and tell no one anything. Are they anticipating the disbelief they would meet in the disciples?

LUKE

The women are Mary Magdalene, Joanna, Mary the mother of James, and other women who had come from Galilee, and all of them had followed and watched the body being laid in the tomb. Then before the Sabbath rest they had prepared spices and perfumed oils (see Luke 23:55-56). So, it is more than three women, but how many?

The women are named at the end of the story, perhaps to keep the emphasis on the *two humans* in shining clothing. Two witnesses would be required for testimony at a trial.

Reminded to remember his words, they begin the remembering that would continue for some time yet of all his words and works. Much of their remembering would be out of natural memory, but how much would be prompted by the Holy Spirit? (see John 14:26)

The *fitting-ness* mentioned in Luke is on both the crucifixion and the rising, while John applies it to the rising again from the dead.

Notice that Peter leaves the disbelieving apostles and runs by himself to the tomb. Take a long prayer walk when you can, imagining an amazed Peter on his walk back to the others.

JOHN

Mary the Magdalene comes to the tomb alone, and runs to report its emptiness without being told to do so. She is therefore known as *the Apostle to the Apostles*, and her July 22nd memorial was "upgraded" in 2016 to a feast!

Mary Magdalene worries about where the body is, first to Peter and the Beloved Disciple. Later she will weep this worry to the two angels, and then a third time to the gardener.

One of the liturgical fights in our time has been where to put the tabernacle in which consecrated hosts are kept to take communion to the sick and homebound. In the 1990s one seminary had moved the tabernacle to a place away from the altar, and a faculty member seeing it said, "They have taken my Lord away, and I do not know where they have put him!" To paraphrase the cable guy comedian, that's funny, I don't care where you are in the liturgy fights.

When Mary the Magdalene says *they took* and *they put*, who does she mean by *they*?

When the Beloved Disciple (here called the *other disciple*) beats Peter in their race to the tomb, having looked in to see the linens, he waits as a kind of key-holder for Peter, who enters first. Still, as the mystic, it is not until he follows Peter into the tomb that he *sees and believes*.

Can you imagine Jesus rising up, letting the linens fall about but taking the cloth from his head to roll up as one would a scroll?

The passage we read on page 9 may be the earliest baptismal creed of the church, but the appearances of the Risen Lord are not part of the Nicene Creed used since 325 A.D., perhaps because Jesus has not shown himself to us in the exact way he did during that first Easter season? Has Jesus shown himself to you?

The Risen Lord has not yet appeared to anyone. If discovering the Empty Tomb were all that happened, would Christianity exist?

FOR PONDERING

Leader Ponder in silence whether in these pages something like one of these surfaced:

a seed planted,
> something I anticipate taking root and growing within me, and growing me…

a memory provoked,
> part of my story or our journey, whether pleasant or sad…

a question raised,
> something unknown
> to study, research, discuss with others, or further ponder…

an action prompted
> or a way to let God grow me into the human person God created me to be…

*Allow another minute for silent pondering,
and then the group may discuss the questions and ponderings
(restraining the urge to "fix" anybody).*

CLOSING PRAYER

When time is up

Leader   Are there any intercessions to offer?

Leader   Let us pray together the Easter Sequence:

All
**Christians, to the Paschal Victim
  Offer your thankful praises!
A Lamb the sheep redeems;
  Christ, who only is sinless,
  Reconciles sinners to the Abba.
Death and life have contended
  in that combat stupendous:
  The Prince of life, who died,
  reigns eternal.
Speak, Mary, declaring
  What you saw, wayfaring.
  "The tomb of Christ, who is living,
    the glory of Jesus' resurrection;
    Bright angels attesting,
    the shroud and napkin resting;
    Yes, Christ my hope is arisen;
    To Galilee he goes before you."
Christ indeed from death is risen,
  our new life obtaining.
  Have mercy, victor Ruler, ever reigning!
  Amen. Alleluia.**

2

MARY MAGDALENE

Leader   Let us sing together as we are able:

All

Ye sons and daugh\-ters of the King,
With heav'n-ly hosts\ in glo\-ry sing,
To-day the grave\ has lost\ its sting:
Al-le-lu-ia!

On that first morn\-ing of\ the week,
Be-fore the day\ be-gan\ to break,
The Ma-rys went\ their Lord\ to seek:
Al-le-lu-ia!

An an-gel bade\ their sor\-row flee,
By speak-ing thus\ un-to\ the three:
"Your Lord is gone\ to Gal\-i-lee:"
Al-le-lu-ia!

Al-le-lu-ia\! Al-le\-lu-ia! Al-le-lu-ia!

> Text: see John 20; attributed to Jean Tisserand, d. 1494;
> translated by John M. Neal, 1851, altered
> Music: 888, O FILII ET FILIAE; Chant Mode II,
> *Airs sur les hymnes sacrez, odes et noels,* 1623

THE RESURRECTION IN THE GREAT STORY OF JESUS 21

Leader Try to notice as we proceed today if
a **seed** is planted,
a **memory** is provoked,
a **question** is raised,
or an **action** is prompted.

Remember that Mary of Magdala is known, we shall see, as *the Apostle to the Apostles*. In 2016 Pope Francis upgraded her memorial day celebrated on each July 22nd to a Feast!

In the Passion story, we are told she is one of the many women who follow Jesus from Galilee and minister to him (see Matthew 27:55).

Because Mark identifies the Magdalene as one cured of seven demons, some of the early scholars misidentified her as the unnamed but publicly known sinner who washed Jesus' feet (see Luke 7:36-50), though that story is more akin to that of the unnamed woman who is not called a sinner who anointed Jesus' feet before he was betrayed (see Mark 14:3-9 & Matthew 26:6-13). Much has been written about this error in our time, but it still shows up in movies, songs, and novels.

Leader Let us take five silent minutes with
Mary Magdalene on the next two pages.

| **MATTHEW** | **MARK** |
| 28:9-10 | 16:9-11 |

9 Behold, Jesus meets them (<u>Mary Magdalene</u> and the other Mary) with, "<u>Greetings!</u>" Approaching they <u>hold his feet</u> and worship him. 10 Jesus says to them, "Be not afraid; <u>Go</u> <u>announce</u> to my brothers that they may go away into Galilee, and there they will see me."	9 Rising early on the first day of the week, <u>he appears first</u> to <u>Mary the Magdalene</u>, from whom he had <u>expelled seven demons</u>. 10 She going reports to <u>those who had been with him</u>, <u>mourning and weeping</u>. 11 Hearing that he is alive and was seen by her, <u>they do not believe</u>.

MATTHEW
28:11-15

11 As they are going,
behold <u>some of the guard</u>
coming into the city <u>tell</u>
<u>all the things</u> that happened
to the chief priests, 12 who
assemble in counsel with the
presbyters and take <u>enough silver</u>
and give it to the guards
13 saying,
"<u>Say</u> that his disciples
  came in the night and stole him
  in your sleep.
14 <u>And if</u> the governor hears this
  we will satisfy him to
  keep you out of trouble."
15 They take the silver
and do as instructed.
And <u>this word is spread</u>
among Judeans to this day.

MARY MAGDALENE

LUKE	JOHN
24:8-12	**20:10-18**

Repeated from	10 The disciples go away again to
The Empty Tomb:	themselves. 11 But <u>Mary</u> stands
	outside the tomb <u>weeping</u>. As she weeps,
8 They remember	she bends into the tomb 12 and behold,
his words, and	<u>two angels</u> in white, sitting, one at the
9 returning from the	head and one at the feet where the body
tomb tell all these things	of Jesus had been. 13 Those say to her,
to the Eleven	"Woman, why do you weep?"
and to all the rest.	She says to them,
10 They are	"<u>They took my Lord</u>, and
<u>*Mary the Magdalene*</u>	<u>I do not know where they put him</u>."
and Joanna and Mary	14 Saying these things, she turns around,
the mother of James,	and behold, Jesus standing.
and the rest with them	She does not know it is Jesus.
who tell these things	15 Jesus says to her,
to the apostles.	"Woman, <u>why do you weep</u>?
11 These words	<u>Whom do you seek</u>?"
seem to them	Thinking it is the <u>gardener</u>,
as folly, and <u>they</u>	she says to him,
<u>*do not believe them*</u>.	"Sir, if you did carry him,
12 But Peter rises,	<u>tell me where you put him</u>,
runs to the tomb...	and I will take him."
	16 Jesus says to her, "Mary."
	Turning, she says to him in Hebrew,
	"Rabboni," which means "Teacher."
	17 Jesus says to her,
	"<u>Do not hold on to me</u>, for I have not yet
	ascended to the Father. But you <u>go</u> to
	my brothers and sisters and <u>tell</u> them,
	'<u>I ascend</u> to my Father and your Father
	and my God and your God.'"
	18 Mary the Magdalene comes
	telling the disciples,
	"<u>I have seen the Lord</u>"
	and these things he said to her.

after five minutes of silence

Leader   We continue taking turns,
reading one paragraph at a time.
Again, if reading in public is not
your thing, just say "pass, please."

Saint Ignatius of Loyola (d. 1556), founder of the Jesuits, contends in his *Spiritual Exercises* that the Risen Jesus appeared first to his mother Mary and then to Mary Magdalene, suggesting that the gospel writers do not tell us this because they assume we already know it.

MATTHEW

The *greeting* given by Jesus is often translated as *Hail!* Jesus would not likely have greeted them in Greek; in any case the word Matthew uses, still used by Greek speakers, means something like *Be joyful!*, as in *Have a joyful day!* Though their names are not spoken, the two Mary's recognize Jesus in the way he greets them, perhaps in recognizing his voice?

Jesus gives the two Mary's instructions for his *brothers*, but though the Eleven will follow these instructions we are not told that the two Mary's told them. In contrast, we are told some of the guard tell the story, and they have to be bribed to tell a lie.

The guards are bribed with *enough silver*; how much would be *enough*? Might it have been the same thirty pieces of silver thrown back into the Temple by Judas? (see Matthew 27:5)

The lie of the guards is spread to the day of the writing of the gospel; does anyone hear it in our day?

MARK

In the other gospels we are given the effects of Jesus rising from the tomb, but in Mark we are told he rises *early* on that first day of the week. Compare this with what happened after Jesus' first long full day of healing: *Rising very early before dawn, he goes out and away to a desert place, and there he prays* (see Mark 1:35).

No words are shared by Jesus and Mary.

It is unclear whether the *mourning and weeping* is by Mary or by the others. They do not believe the news from her; perhaps Jesus sent her to help get them ready to accept his appearances without freaking out.

Would you have believed this news from Mary Magdalene? If not, what preparation might have gotten you ready for it?

LUKE

Nowhere in Luke are we told Jesus appears to Mary Magdalene. Some have suggested she could be the unnamed disciple on the road to Emmas, but this is unlikely as we will see in the next chapter that the two on the road will have received the report from the women who go to the tomb early.

The women (Mary Magdalene, Joanna, Mary the mother of James, and other women who had come from Galilee) believe the two men at least partly because they quote them some of Jesus' own words. All of them tell these things to the apostles, who consider it as folly and nonsense. And yet, again, Peter is at least curious enough to run to the tomb.

Notice also that at this point (only in Luke) Jesus has still not yet shown himself to anyone.

JOHN

Peter and the Beloved Disciple leave, but Mary Magdalene stays at the tomb. Is she sensing a holy place or a holy presence?

Mary speaks her concerns over the whereabouts of the body of Jesus three times, first to Peter and the Beloved Disciple, then to the two angels in the tomb, and then again to Jesus whom she mistakes for the gardener. Jesus questions her about her weeping, as he is about to overwhelm her with good news. And he asks her whom she seeks, the question he had posed to the powers at his arrest (see John 18:4).

Mentioning a *gardener* can awaken our memory of Adam and Eve in the garden of paradise, where God also asks a question while knowing the answer: *Who told you that you were naked?* (see Genesis 3:11)

Mary is alone with Jesus, so here Jesus greets her by saying her name, *Mary*. She is intimate enough with Jesus to recognize him by the way he says her name.

She answers with her name for him, *Rabboni*, while *turning*, a word that can signify a conversion happening.

There is some kind of power in knowing someone's name.

As in Matthew, Mary holds on to Jesus, who begins preparing her for the letting-go they will all experience in the Ascension.

When she does tell the disciples, *I have seen the Lord*, John does not give us their response.

FOR PONDERING

Leader Ponder in silence whether in these pages something like one of these surfaced:

a seed planted,
> something I anticipate taking root and growing within me, and growing me…

a memory provoked,
> part of my story or our journey, whether pleasant or sad…

a question raised,
> something unknown
> to study, research, discuss with others, or further ponder…

an action prompted
> or a way to let God grow me into the human person God created me to be…

*Allow another minute for silent pondering,
and then the group may discuss the questions and ponderings
(restraining the urge to "fix" anybody).*

CLOSING PRAYER

When time is up

Leader Are there any intercessions to offer?

Leader Let us pray together the Easter Sequence:

All
**Christians, to the Paschal Victim
   Offer your thankful praises!
A Lamb the sheep redeems;
   Christ, who only is sinless,
   Reconciles sinners to the Abba.
Death and life have contended
   in that combat stupendous:
   The Prince of life, who died,
   reigns eternal.
Speak, Mary, declaring
   What you saw, wayfaring.
   "The tomb of Christ, who is living,
     the glory of Jesus' resurrection;
     Bright angels attesting,
     the shroud and napkin resting;
     Yes, Christ my hope is arisen;
     To Galilee he goes before you."
Christ indeed from death is risen,
   our new life obtaining.
   Have mercy, victor Ruler, ever reigning!
   Amen. Alleluia.**

3

THE ROAD TO EMMAUS

Leader   Let us sing together as we are able:

All

I know that my Re/-deem-er\ lives;
What com-fort this sweet sen-tence gives!
Liv-ing\ Proph/-et/, Priest\, and\ King;
Liv-ing a-live, and so I sing.

He lives/ hun-gry/ souls to\ feed,
Liv-ing to help in time of need.
Liv-ing to grant/ us/ rich\ sup\-ply,
Liv-ing to guide us with his eye.

He lives/ qui-et/ing our\ fears,
Liv-ing to wipe a-way our tears,
Liv-ing to calm/ our/ troubl\-ed\ heart,
Liv-ing all bless-ings to im-part.

He lives/, glo-ry/ to his\ Name!
Liv-ing, my Je-sus, still the same.
Oh, sweet the joy/ this/ sen\-tence\ gives:
"I know that my Re-deem-er lives!"

Text: from Job 19:25-27, Samuel Medley, 1775, altered
Music: DUKE STREET, LM, John Hatton, 1793
Popular melody for: *From All That Dwells Below The Skies*

Leader Try to notice as we proceed today if
a **seed** is planted,
a **memory** is provoked,
a **question** is raised,
or an **action** is prompted.

In *Mark* we are given a much condensed version of the Emmaus appearance.

Only in *Luke* do we hear the details of it. Notice the dance of the Sunday Eucharist:

1st - They are in the presence of Jesus, in the same way that Jesus still gathers us together.

2nd - Jesus recounts and expounds on the story they already know of salvation history, just as we celebrate the Liturgy of the Word.

3rd - At table Jesus breaks the bread with them and they recognize him in a mysterious presence and invisibility, an intimate encounter with Christ the Risen Lord.

4th - They know they are sent back to the others, just as we too are sent on mission to carry the presence of Christ into the world.

Let us take five silent minutes on the Road to Emmaus on the next two pages.

MARK
16:12-13

12 After these things, to <u>two of them walking</u>
he <u>shows himself</u> in <u>a different form</u>, going into the country.
13 Those going tell the rest, and are <u>not believed</u>.

LUKE
24:13-35

13 Behold, <u>two of them</u> on the same day
are <u>journeying</u> to a village named Emmaus,
sixty stadia (7 miles) distant from Jerusalem,
14 and they are talking to each other
about all these things having occurred.
15 As they talk and discuss,
<u>Jesus himself drawing near journeys with them</u>,
16 but their eyes are <u>held to not</u> recognize him.
17 He says to them, "What are
 these words you exchange with each other as you walk?"
They stand with <u>sad faces</u>.
18 The one named <u>Cleopas</u> answering says,
"You are only a <u>stranger</u> in Jerusalem and do not know
 the things happening there <u>in these days</u>?"
19 He says to them,
"What things?"
And they say to him,
"The things about Jesus the Nazarene,
 who was a <u>prophet-human</u>,
 <u>powerful in work and word</u> before God and all the people,
 20 how both the chief priests and our rulers
 delivered him to judgment of death and crucified him.
 21 <u>We were hoping</u> that he was the one about to <u>redeem</u> Israel.
 Also with all these things,
 <u>this is the third day</u> since these things happened.
 22 But also <u>some of our women amazed us</u>.
 Being at the tomb early 23 and not finding his body,
 they came saying they had seen a <u>vision of angels</u>
 who say that he is alive.

THE ROAD TO EMMAUS

24 Some of the ones with us went to the tomb,
and found as indeed the women said,
but <u>him they did not see</u>."
25 He says to them,
"<u>How dense</u> you are and <u>slow in heart</u> to believe
in all things which the prophets spoke.
26 Did <u>the Messiah (Christ)</u> not deem it <u>fitting</u>
to <u>suffer these things</u> and to enter into his <u>glory</u>?"
27 Beginning from Moses and from all the prophets,
he explains to them in all the scriptures
the things concerning himself.

28 <u>As they draw near</u>
to the village to which they are journeying,
he pretends to journey farther.
29 They urge him saying,
"<u>Stay with us</u>, because it is near evening
and the day has declined."
He goes in to stay with them.
30 As he reclines at table with them, <u>taking</u> the bread,
he <u>blesses</u>, and having <u>broken</u> he <u>hands</u> it to them.
31 Their eyes are opened and they recognize him;
and he <u>becomes invisible</u> to them.

32 They say to each other,
"Were not <u>our hearts burning</u> in us
as he spoke to us on the way,
as he opened up to us the scriptures?
33 <u>Rising up</u> in the same hour,
they return to Jerusalem
and <u>find the Eleven collected</u>
and the ones with them 34 saying,
"Truly the Lord is risen
and <u>appeared to Simon</u>."
35 They relate <u>the things on the way</u>
and how he was <u>known by them</u>
in the <u>breaking of the bread</u>.

after five minutes of silence

Leader We continue taking turns,
reading one paragraph at a time.
Again, if reading in public is not
your thing, just say "pass, please."

MARK

Jesus *shows himself* to two walking into the country, and they are not believed when they tell the others. These are two of *those who had been with him*, his *companions*, who had not believed Mary Magdalene.

They know it is him even though he shows himself in a *different form*. Can you imagine it.

Jesus shows himself to people who already know him, who have enough history with him to recognize him, even in a new form.

LUKE

If you want to guess who the *two of them* are, pick up your Bible and run down that rabbit hole. One is named *Cleopas*, who shows up nowhere else in the gospels, though in John the wife of a *Clopas* stood by the cross with Jesus' mother, the sister of his mother, and Mary Magdalene (see John 19:25). Following Luke alone, one could be one of the unnumbered women from Galilee who encountered the two men in shining clothing; neither are apostles.

We can ask Cleopas in heaven who was with him or her, but perhaps it is best to pray the story as yourself being one of the two.

In one discussion group with this material a woman challenged that "nowhere in the Bible does it say a woman is a disciple." Is this correct?

Does Jesus go to them because they are walking away from his mission? Is it to reunite them with the others? Is it to use them as well as Mary Magdalene to soften the ground for the shock of his upcoming appearance to the others?

People only see what they're prepared to see. (Ralph Waldo Emerson) They were not expecting to see Jesus. Are the two kept from recognizing Jesus so that he can also prepare them for the recognition to come at the meal?

When their conversation is interrupted their faces are sad. This is why we often avoid silence by keeping the talking going. Does *stand with sad faces* mean that their walking journey is halted for a moment?

They tell what they know about Jesus, the powerful prophet in whom they had found the hope of their redemption. Being redeemed is as being ransomed out of prison, as for example were both Francis of Assisi and Ignatius of Loyola. Whom could you count on to pay a ransom to get you set free?

The story is already changing, as stories do in the retelling: the women saw *two humans*, but the two journeyers report *a vision of angels*.

Almost reaching their destination, they invite the stranger to stay with them. Has Jesus somehow invited them to invite him into their home? Perhaps the *Wow* of the *burning of their heart* prompted the invitation. Hospitality was demanded in the Jewish culture, but we don't break bread with just anybody.

The bread is taken, blessed, broken, and given, just as in the multiplication of loaves (see Luke 9:10-17). This is the dance of the Eucharist. If the event is in the 30s A.D., and Luke is written in the 80s A.D., then there have already been about fifty years of the Church tradition of celebrating the Sunday Eucharist.

When they recognize him he vanishes from their sight, but not necessarily from their presence. Just because we cannot see Jesus does not mean he is not there.

The bread is broken, but we are not told that they eat anything. And yet they have been nourished enough to make the return trip right away.

Their *rising up* from the table is resurrection language.

When they return to the Eleven still in Jerusalem, they are told the Risen Lord has appeared to Simon. Perhaps this was during his walk home from the tomb, amazed.

So far, Jesus has been recognized by Mary Magdalene (in Matthew, Mark & John), Mary the mother of James and Joseph (in Matthew), Simon Peter (in Luke), and Cleopas and his or her companion (also in Luke).

Could he have also appeared to others without their being able to recognize him? What about us?

FOR PONDERING

Leader Ponder in silence whether in these pages something like one of these surfaced:

a seed planted,
> something I anticipate taking root and growing within me, and growing me…

a memory provoked,
> part of my story or our journey, whether pleasant or sad…

a question raised,
> something unknown
> to study, research, discuss with others, or further ponder…

an action prompted
> or a way to let God grow me into the human person God created me to be…

*Allow another minute for silent pondering,
and then the group may discuss the questions and ponderings
(restraining the urge to "fix" anybody).*

CLOSING PRAYER

When time is up

Leader Are there any intercessions to offer?

Leader Let us pray together the Easter Sequence:

All
**Christians, to the Paschal Victim
  Offer your thankful praises!
A Lamb the sheep redeems;
  Christ, who only is sinless,
  Reconciles sinners to the Abba.
Death and life have contended
  in that combat stupendous:
  The Prince of life, who died,
  reigns eternal.
Speak, Mary, declaring
  What you saw, wayfaring.
  "The tomb of Christ, who is living,
    the glory of Jesus' resurrection;
    Bright angels attesting,
    the shroud and napkin resting;
    Yes, Christ my hope is arisen;
    To Galilee he goes before you."
Christ indeed from death is risen,
  our new life obtaining.
  Have mercy, victor Ruler, ever reigning!
  Amen. Alleluia.**

4

THE UPPER ROOM

Leader   Let us sing together as we are able:

All

That night th'A-pos\-tles met\ in fear,
A-midst them came\ their Lord\ most dear
And said, "Peace be\ un-to\ you here:"
Al-le-lu-ia!

Bless-ed are they\ that have\ not seen
And yet whose faith\ has con\-stant been,
In life e-ter\-nal they\ shall reign:
Al-le-lu-ia!

And we with ho\-ly Church\ u-nite,
As ev-er-more\ is just\ and right,
In glo-ry to\ the Rul-er of light:
Al-le-lu-ia!

Al-le-lu-ia\! Al-le\-lu-ia! Al-le-lu-ia!

> Text: see John 20; attributed to Jean Tisserand, d. 1494;
> translated by John M. Neal, 1851, altered
> Music: 888, O FILII ET FILIAE; Chant Mode II,
> *Airs sur les hymnes sacrez, odes et noels*, 1623

THE RESURRECTION IN THE GREAT STORY OF JESUS

Leader Try to notice as we proceed today if
a **seed** is planted,
a **memory** is provoked,
a **question** is raised,
or an **action** is prompted.

In Mark, when it was time for the Passover, Jesus sent two of his disciples into the city to follow a man carrying a water jar, to say to the master of the house he enters, "The Teacher says, *where is the guestroom where I may eat the Passover with my disciples?*," and to make the preparations in the already furnished **large upper room** they will be shown.

Peter and John are named in Luke as those two disciples. Matthew omits the water jar and has all the disciples making the preparations. John doesn't speak about the preparations, but only in John are we told of a door in a room where Jesus shows himself.

All of this keeps the identity of Jesus' host unknown. In the movies this is the same room where Jesus appears to the apostles together.

Let us take five silent minutes in the Upper Room on the next two pages.

MARK	LUKE	Easter B-3
16:14	24:36-45	24:35-45

MARK	LUKE

14 Later to the Eleven
as they recline at table
he shows himself
and reproaches them
for their disbelief
and their hardness of heart
for not believing
the ones who saw him
after being risen.
	36 These things being said by
	them, he stands in their midst
	and says to them,
	"Peace to you."
	37 Startled and terrified,
	they think they behold a spirit.
	38 He says to them,
	"Why are you troubled?
	  Why do doubts arise
	  in your hearts?
	39 See my hands and my feet,
	  that I am myself.
	  Touch me and see, because
	  a spirit has no flesh or bones
	  as you behold me having."
	40 Saying this, he shows them
	his hands and his feet.
	41 Yet disbelieving from
	their joy and amazement,
	he says to them,
	"Have you any food here?"
	42 They hand to him
	a piece of broiled fish.
	43 Taking he eats before them.
	44 He says to them,
	"These my words I spoke to you
	  while yet with you,
	  of the need to be fulfilled
	  of all things written
	  concerning me
	  in the law of Moses
	  and the Prophets
	  and the Psalms."
	45 Then he opens up
	their minds to understand
	the scriptures.

JOHN
20:19-31   Second Sunday of Easter ABC

19 When it is early evening on that day one of the week,
the doors having been <u>locked</u> where the disciples are
because of <u>fear</u> of the Judeans,
Jesus comes and stands in the midst and says to them,
  "<u>Peace to you</u>."
20 Saying this he shows both <u>his hands and his side</u> to them,
so the disciples <u>seeing</u> the Lord <u>rejoice</u>.
21 Jesus says to them again,
"<u>Peace to you</u>; as the Father has sent me, I also send you."
22 Saying this he <u>breathes</u> in and <u>onto them</u> saying,
"<u>Receive Holy Spirit</u>.
23 Of whomever you forgive the sins, they are <u>forgiven</u> of them;
  of whomever you hold, they are <u>held</u>."

24 But <u>Thomas</u>, one of the twelve called Twin,
is not with them when Jesus comes.
25 So the other disciples say to him, "We have seen the Lord."
But he says to them,
"<u>Unless I see</u> in his hands the <u>mark of the nails</u> and put
my finger into the place of the nails and put <u>my hand into his side</u>,
by no means will I believe."
26 After <u>eight days</u>, again his disciples are within,
and Thomas is with them.
The <u>doors</u> having been <u>locked</u>,
Jesus comes and stands in the midst and says,
"<u>Peace to you</u>."
27 Then he says to Thomas, "<u>Bring your finger here</u>
  and <u>see my hands</u>, and bring and put your hand <u>into my side</u>,
  and be not unbelieving, but believe."
28 Thomas answers and says to him, "<u>My Lord and my God</u>."
29 Jesus says to him,
"You believe because you have seen me.
  Blessed are the ones not seeing and yet believing."

30 Jesus does <u>many and other signs</u> in the presence of the disciples
which have not been written in this scroll. 31 But <u>these have been
written</u> that you may believe that Jesus is the Christ, the Son of God,
and that believing you may have life in his name.

after five minutes of silence

Leader We continue taking turns,
reading one paragraph at a time.
Again, if reading in public is not
your thing, just say "pass, please."

MATTHEW

As instructed by Jesus through Mary Magdalene and Mary the mother of James and Joseph, the Eleven disciples will not see Jesus until they return to Galilee. See Chapter 6.

MARK

Jesus meets them in their meal and in their rest, and literally *shows himself*.

He challenges them to trust one another's telling of the Easter story. Sometimes we dismiss our own religious experiences out of fear of being disbelieved, made fun of, or thought crazy. Jesus wants us to share these things with each other, for the good of all.

When my dad Charlie Wolf would hear things of faith that some might think crazy, he would silently lean his head a bit to one side, shrug his shoulders and turn his palms up, as if to say, *Could be, doesn't have to be, but could be.*

All the appearances of the Risen Lord call on the senses of sight and sound, but Luke and John also draw on the sense of touch.

LUKE

It is while the two have returned from Emmaus and are telling their story to the Eleven that Jesus *stands in their midst*, not to interrupt their telling but to punctuate it.

Jesus acknowledges that they are troubled and shows them his own wounds, as if to say *Look at what they did to me*. Though he is risen, he still carries the wounds. So will we.

The complex reaction of the Eleven is disbelief and joy and marveling. In response Jesus asks for something to eat, giving them the opportunity to serve him and the time it takes to calm down.

He asks for food, just as he had asked that the daughter of Jairus be given something to eat after her breath returned (See Luke 8:55).

He eats what they have to offer, as he had taught the 72 he sent on mission (see Luke 10:7).

Is he famished, or did he eat just a bite? Fish will also be part of the breakfast in Galilee as told in John.

Jesus also shows himself in the scriptures that they already know: the Torah (the Law or first five books), the Prophets, and the Psalms.

Their minds are opened by Jesus. Our understanding is itself a gift of Jesus.

JOHN

They are hiding in fear behind locked doors. Between the two blessings of *Peace to you*, Jesus shows them his wounded hands and side. Are they afraid that like Jesus they might also be crucified? Or are they afraid that Jesus who knows they abandoned him (all except his mother, her sister, Mary of Clopas, Mary Magdalene, and the Beloved Disciple) has been seen? Would it not be reasonable for them to think he might be angry with them? And Peter had denied knowing him three times!

Jesus is not angry. He breathes onto them the Holy Spirit, the Holy Breath, and tells them to receive the Holy Spirit and with this breath the power to forgive. And the power to not forgive. In his ministry, forgiveness of sins is the greatest gift Jesus gives.

God creates humanity, breathing the breath of life into *'adam*. We suffocate the *New Adam* on the cross. And God's response to that is to breath the Holy Breath of mercy into us.

This can be seen as John's explanation of the coming of the Holy Spirit, which we set side-by-side with Luke's story in the beginning of the Book of Acts.

Thomas is not with them the first time, and so does not believe. He is the only one in John who does not believe, while in the other gospels pretty much no one believes until they see. And Jesus rebukes them.

Thomas is the source of all our FOMO (fear of missing out) Where was he that night? Getting food? Out for some fresh air? To the latrine? Checking in on somebody else?

Thomas is in this state of disbelief for an entire week. Perhaps he is jealous of what the others have seen and heard. Perhaps he has been lied to once too often. Perhaps he is one of those folks who calmly insist on evidence.

Jesus' invitation to touch him carries a close intimacy, as if he is saying, *Enter my side*. We are not told whether Thomas touches Jesus, but he gives us a beautiful prayer of faith, *My Lord and my God* (perhaps from Psalm 5:3). Here is a great mantra to breathe on an Easter walk.

FOR PONDERING

Leader Ponder in silence whether in these pages something like one of these surfaced:

a seed planted,
> something I anticipate taking root and growing within me, and growing me…

a memory provoked,
> part of my story or our journey, whether pleasant or sad…

a question raised,
> something unknown
> to study, research, discuss with others, or further ponder…

an action prompted
> or a way to let God grow me into the human person God created me to be…

Allow another minute for silent pondering, and then the group may discuss the questions and ponderings (restraining the urge to "fix" anybody).

CLOSING PRAYER

When time is up

Leader   Are there any intercessions to offer?

Leader   Let us pray together the Easter Sequence:

All
**Christians, to the Paschal Victim
   Offer your thankful praises!
A Lamb the sheep redeems;
   Christ, who only is sinless,
   Reconciles sinners to the Abba.
Death and life have contended
   in that combat stupendous:
   The Prince of life, who died,
   reigns eternal.
Speak, Mary, declaring
   What you saw, wayfaring.
   "The tomb of Christ, who is living,
     the glory of Jesus' resurrection;
     Bright angels attesting,
     the shroud and napkin resting;
     Yes, Christ my hope is arisen;
     To Galilee he goes before you."
Christ indeed from death is risen,
   our new life obtaining.
   Have mercy, victor Ruler, ever reigning!
   Amen. Alleluia.**

5

THE SEASHORE BREAKFAST

Leader   Let us sing together as we are able:

All

Let us break bread to-geth-er on our knees;
Let us break bread to-geth-er on our knees;
When I fall on my knees,
With my face to the ris-ing sun,
O/ Lord, have mer-cy on_ me.

Let us drink wine to-geth-er on our knees;
Let us drink wine to-geth-er on our knees;
When I fall on my knees,
With my face to the ris-ing sun,
O/ Lord, have mer-cy on_ me.

Let us praise God to-geth-er on our knees;
Let us praise God to-geth-er on our knees;
When I fall on my knees,
With my face to the ris-ing sun,
O/ Lord, have mer-cy on_ me.

Text: Spiritual
Music: 10 10 with refrain
LET US BREAK BREAD, Spiritual

THE RESURRECTION IN THE GREAT STORY OF JESUS 51

Leader Try to notice as we proceed today if
 a **seed** is planted,
 a **memory** is provoked,
 a **question** is raised,
 or an **action** is prompted.

This breakfast story appears only in *John*, though there is another story of a miraculous catch of fish in Luke 5, which also is focused on Simon, who is told by Jesus he will be a fisher of people. In both of these stories the fisher is converted into a shepherd.

The Greek word for fish (IXTHUS) was an early code word for Christians living under threat of being persecuted. Ἰησοῦς Χριστός Θεοῦ Υἱός Σωτήρ, pronounced today *Iēsoûs Khrīstós, Theoû Huiós Sōtḗr*, is translated *Jesus Christ, Son of God and Savior*. Seen the fish on any cars or trucks lately?

Let us take five silent minutes at the Seashore Breakfast on the next two pages.

JOHN
21:1-19 Easter C-3

1 After these things Jesus again <u>shows himself</u> to the disciples
at the sea of Tiberias, and he shows himself thus:
2 There are together <u>Simon Peter</u> and <u>Thomas</u>, called Twin,
and <u>Nathanael</u> from Cana of Galilee, and the <u>sons of Zebedee</u>,
and <u>two others</u> of the disciples.
3 Simon Peter says to them,
  "<u>I am going to fish</u>."
They say to him,
  "We also are coming with you."
<u>They go forth</u> and embark in the boat,
and in that night they <u>catch nothing</u>.

4 When it <u>the day breaks</u>, Jesus stands on the shore;
however, the disciples do not know that it is Jesus.
5 Jesus says to them,
  "Children, have you not any fish?"
They answer him, "No."
6 He says to them,
  "<u>Cast the net</u> on the right side of the boat,
   and you will find."
They cast, and they are unable to drag in
from the <u>multitude</u> of the fishes.
7 <u>The disciple whom Jesus loves</u> says to Peter,
  "<u>It is the Lord</u>."
Simon Peter, hearing that it is the Lord,
girds himself with his garment, for he is naked,
and <u>casts himself</u> into the sea.
8 The other disciples come in the little boat,
for they are not far from land, about two hundred cubits (100 yards),
dragging the net of the fishes.
9 When they disembark onto the land,
they see a <u>coal fire</u> and a <u>fish</u> lying and <u>bread</u> lying.
10 Jesus says to them,
  "Bring from the fishes you caught now."
11 Simon Peter goes up and drags the net to the land,
full of <u>a hundred</u> <u>fifty-three mega fish</u>,
and being so many the net is not torn.

THE SEASHORE BREAKFAST

12 Jesus says to them,
  "<u>Come, you; break the fast</u>."
Not one of the disciples dare to question him, "who are you,"
knowing that it is the Lord.
13 Jesus comes and takes the bread and gives it to them,
and the fish likewise.
14 This is now the third time
that Jesus <u>shows himself</u> to the <u>disciples</u> after rising from the dead.

15 When they have breakfasted, Jesus says to Simon Peter,
  "Simon of John, do you <u>*agape*-love</u> me more than these?"
He says to him,
  "Yes, Lord, you know that I <u>*philia*-love</u> you."
He says to him,
  "<u>Feed my lambs</u>."

16 He says to him again secondly,
  "Simon of John, do you <u>*agape*-love</u> me?"
He says to him,
  "Yes, Lord, you know that I <u>*philia*-love</u> you."
He says to him,
  "<u>Shepherd my sheep</u>."

17 He says to him the third,
  "Simon of John, do you <u>*philia*-love</u> me?"
Peter is grieved that he said to him the third 'do you love me?'
and says to him,
  "Lord, you know all things, you know that I <u>*philia*-love</u> you."
Jesus says to him,
  "<u>Feed my sheep</u>.

18 Amen amen I tell you,
   when you were younger, you girded yourself
   and walked where you wished;
     but <u>when you grow old</u>, you will stretch out your hands
   and another will gird you and will carry you
   where you do not wish."
19 This he says signifying by what death he will glorify God.
Saying this he tells him,
  "<u>Follow me</u>."

after five minutes of silence

Leader We continue taking turns,
reading one paragraph at a time.
Again, if reading in public is not
your thing, just say "pass, please."

JOHN

What leads Simon Peter to go fishing? Is he considering returning to his old way of life, his old vocation? Does he miss fishing? Is he bored? Is he getting tired of waiting for Jesus? Is he hungry? Has he simply gotta do something?

When they go fishing without being sent they catch nothing. When Jesus tells them to cast, they do not argue even though they do not yet know it is him; they just do it.

The miracle is so big it is difficult to deal with the results.

The mystic, the Beloved Disciple, sees that a miracle has happened and so says, *It is the Lord*, the same one who had stepped into the tomb, saw, and believed.

Simon, who is Peter because of Jesus, impetuously gets dressed to throw or *cast* himself into the water, as if he is to be used by Jesus as bait.

The fish are big, bringing to mind the story of Jonah. The number *153* is thought to be the number of kinds of fish or the number of nations at the time.

If the net represents the Church, it is big, and it does not tear; it is meant to stretch.

This is the third time in John that Jesus *shows himself to the disciples* as a group. It is in the context of a meal, for Jesus has cooked up a breakfast. The time of fasting is over, for the Christ is with them.

Jesus *takes* and *gives* the bread and the fish to them. Remember that like the other gospels John was written for a community already with a tradition of celebrating the Eucharist.

Fish can signify the traveling the Church would do. But why don't we do Sunday Eucharist with fish? Is fish just too messy? Is it from the role of bread in the Passover meal? Is it that bread and wine are from both the goods of creation and the work of human beings?

Having called them to *break the fast*, there seems to be silence through the meal, no questions nor any conversation until Jesus breaks the silence. In our time, conversation often happens while we eat, though when the situation is uncomfortable some of us eat more and some of us less. Is Jesus comfortable in the silence, hoping to put them at ease? Perhaps small talk is simply out of the question. Does Jesus wait politely until they are satiated before speaking again?

Jesus' triple questioning allows Simon to make a triple affirmation to reverse his earlier triple denial of Jesus. That Peter *grieves* can suggest he internalizes this new affirmation, even forgiving himself. This happens at a charcoal fire, as did Simon's earlier denial.

In the first question Jesus asks if Simon loves him *more than these*. The question can be heard and answered in different ways: More than the miracle of the catch of fish? More than the other disciples love Jesus? More than Simon loves the other disciples?

Jesus asks twice for *agape*-love, the highest form, but when Simon answers with *philia*-love, or brotherly love, Jesus finally accepts the *philia*-love Simon is able to give. Do we say by the way we live, *Sure, Lord, I love you as a bro*.

The gospels are written in Greek, and *agape* and *philia* are Greek words unlikely to have been used by Jesus, and yet distinctive words that would have been understood by the first hearers of what we call the gospel of John.

Jesus calls him to *feed my lambs*, to *shepherd my sheep*, and then to *feed my sheep*. A lamb needs baby food; a sheep needs grown-up food. But shepherding is more than just feeding; the call is also to watch over the sheep as they mature and into maturity.

In all three instructions, the sheep are *my sheep*, so Jesus' sheep.

Does *the disciple whom Jesus loves*, whom tradition treats as John of Zebedee and the author of this gospel, seem to enjoy telling about Jesus asking Simon these love questions?

Would you want to be told by Jesus how your death will happen in the same way he tells Simon?

When Jesus concludes the breakfast with the words *follow me*, is that more comforting or more challenging to you?

Alleluia in Greek, *Hallelujah* in Hebrew, mean *Praise God!* Saint Augustine of Hippo wrote, *We are an Easter people, and Alleluia is our song!* What does it mean for you to be an Easter person? Is that different from being part of an Easter people?

FOR PONDERING

Leader Ponder in silence whether in these pages something like one of these surfaced:

a seed planted,
   something I anticipate taking root and growing within me, and growing me...

a memory provoked,
   part of my story or our journey, whether pleasant or sad...

a question raised,
   something unknown
   to study, research, discuss with others, or further ponder...

an action prompted
   or a way to let God grow me into the human person God created me to be...

*Allow another minute for silent pondering,
and then the group may discuss the questions and ponderings
(restraining the urge to "fix" anybody).*

CLOSING PRAYER

When time is up

Leader Are there any intercessions to offer?

Leader Let us pray together the Easter Sequence:

All
**Christians, to the Paschal Victim
   Offer your thankful praises!
A Lamb the sheep redeems;
   Christ, who only is sinless,
   Reconciles sinners to the Abba.
Death and life have contended
   in that combat stupendous:
   The Prince of life, who died,
   reigns eternal.
Speak, Mary, declaring
   What you saw, wayfaring.
   "The tomb of Christ, who is living,
     the glory of Jesus' resurrection;
     Bright angels attesting,
     the shroud and napkin resting;
     Yes, Christ my hope is arisen;
     To Galilee he goes before you."
Christ indeed from death is risen,
   our new life obtaining.
   Have mercy, victor Ruler, ever reigning!
   Amen. Alleluia.**

6

THE GREAT COMMISSION
THE ASCENSION
THE BELOVED DISCIPLE

Leader   Let us sing together as we are able:

All

In/ Christ there is no/ East or West,
In him no South\ or/ North;
But/ one com-mu-nion of God's love
Through/-out/ the whole\ wide earth.

In/ Christ shall true hearts/ ev-'ry-where
Their high vo-ca\-tion/ find;
His/ ser-vice is the gold-en cord,
Close/ bind/-ing hu\-man-kind.

In/ Christ now meet both/ East and West,
In him meet South\ and/ North;
All/ souls of Christ are one in him
Through/-out/ the whole\ wide earth.

> Text: see Galatians 3:8, William A. Dunkerley, 1908,
> under the pseudonym of John Oxenham, altered
> Music: MCKEE, CM; African American Spiritual,
> arranged by Harry T. Burleigh, 1866-1949

THE RESURRECTION IN THE GREAT STORY OF JESUS 61

Leader Try to notice as we proceed today if
a **seed** is planted,
a **memory** is provoked,
a **question** is raised,
or an **action** is prompted.

Leader   John 21:25

A reading from the gospel of John:

There are also many other things Jesus does, which if they were written singly, I think not the cosmos itself would contain the bibles being written.

The gospel of the Lord.
All **Praise to you, Lord Jesus Christ.**

Leader Hear this comment from one who sat for six weeks with these four narratives:

It's as if four people heard the same poem and shared with others the essence of the poem and those different groups of hearers somehow got together and shared the poem with each other.

Let us take five silent minutes with the Ascension on the next two pages.

THE GREAT COMMISSION — THE ASCENSION

MATTHEW
28:16-20   Ascension A

16 <u>The Eleven</u> disciples
go to Galilee to <u>the mountain
where Jesus directed them</u>.
17 Seeing him they worship,
but some doubt.
18 Approaching,
Jesus talks with them saying,
"<u>All authority</u>
 in heaven and on earth
 has been given to me.
19 So, <u>go</u>,
 make disciples
 of <u>all the nations</u>,
 baptizing them
 <u>in the name of the Father
 and of the Son
 and of the Holy Spirit</u>,
20 teaching them
 to observe all things
 that I commanded you.
 And <u>behold</u>
 <u>I am with you always</u>,
 all the days until
 the end of the eon."

MARK
16:15-20   Ascension B

15 He says to them,
"<u>Go</u> into all the cosmos,
 <u>proclaim the gospel
 to all creation</u>.
16 The one <u>believing</u>
 and being <u>baptized</u>
 will be <u>saved</u>,
 but the one not believing
 will be condemned.
17 <u>These signs</u> will follow
 the ones believing:
 In my name
 they will expel <u>demons</u>,
 they will speak
 with new <u>tongues</u>,
18 they will pick up <u>serpents</u>,
 and if they <u>drink</u> anything
 deadly by no means
 will it hurt them,
 and they will lay <u>hands on
 the sick</u> who will recover."
19 So the Lord Jesus
after speaking to them
is <u>taken up into heaven</u> and
<u>sits at the right hand of God</u>.
20 Those going forth
<u>proclaim everywhere</u>,
while the Lord works with them
and confirms the word
through accompanying signs.

THE ASCENSION

LUKE
24:46-53 Ascension C

46 He says to them,
"Thus it has been written:
  the Messiah (Christ) to suffer
  and to rise out of the dead
  on the third day,
  and in his name
47 a proclamation of repentance
  into forgiveness of sin,
  to all the nations
  beginning from Jerusalem.
48 You are witnesses
of these things.
49 And behold
  I send forth on you
  the promise of my Father,
  but sit in the city
  until you are clothed
  out of the height with power."
50 He leads them
out to Bethany,
and lifting up his hands
he blesses them.
51 While he blesses them
he withdraws from them.
and is carried up to heaven
52 They worship him
and return to Jerusalem
with mega joy,
53 and are constantly
in the temple blessing God.

THE BELOVED DISCIPLE

JOHN
21:20-23

20 Turning, Peter sees following
the disciple whom Jesus loves,
who had leaned on his breast
at the supper saying 'Lord
who is betraying you?'
21 Seeing this one,
Peter says to Jesus,
"Lord, what of this one?"
22 Jesus says to him,
"If I wish him to remain
  until I come, what to you?
  You, follow me."
23 So this word goes forth
to the brothers and sisters
that this disciple does not die;
but Jesus did not say he
would not die, but:
"If I wish him to remain
  until I come, what to you?"

JOHN
21:24-25

24 This is the disciple
witnessing these things and
having written these things,
and we know that
his witness is true.
25 There are also
many other things Jesus does,
which if they were
written singly,
I think not the cosmos itself
would contain the bibles
being written.

after five minutes of silence

Leader   We continue taking turns,
reading one paragraph at a time.
Again, if reading in public is not
your thing, just say "pass, please."

MATTHEW

The Eleven go to the mountain in Galilee as reported to them by Mary Magdalene and Mary the mother of James and Joseph.

Some of the Eleven doubt, but this does not seem to challenge or bother Jesus in the least.

There is no Ascension. We are told rather about *the Great Commission*, to go to the nations to baptize in what has come to be known as the trinitarian formula (Father, Son and Holy Spirit) and to teach and do what Jesus has taught.

Jesus also gives us the consoling promise *Behold I am with you always*. A similar *presence prayer* can be used by parents for children and when folks approach but do not receive holy communion, *May God be with you always*.

MARK

The Great Commission is to go, and to tell the

good news to all of creation, leaving the hearers then with a choice, to *believe* (which with being *baptized* leads to being *saved*) or to *disbelieve* (leading to *condemnation*).

Have you been saved? Might a Catholic respond, *we're all working on it together*?

It's up to you whether to take the *accompanying signs* literally. The comedian Jerry Clower claimed he found himself inside a church building filled with snakes and snake handlers, and when told there was no back door exclaimed, *Howw! Where do ya want one?*

Is there ever a sign that faith has an effect in the cosmos? Ever heard of demons expelled? Ask an addict who has found sobriety after compulsions and addictions had stolen their freedom, and how that came to be.

Do you ever *speak with new tongues*? Ask someone who has been graced to overcome an intractable conflict by the capacity to really listen, truly hear the other, and even learn to speak the other's language.

Do you ever *take serpents* or *drink deadly things*? Ask anyone who has overcome a disabling fear of things that used to scare them into a frozen deadness.

Do you ever *lay hands* on the sick in a way that heals them? Or does anyone ever *lay hands* on you in a way that heals you. Besides those who have received the charism of healing, human beings often bring healing to one another with the gift of touch.

After Jesus is *taken up into heaven* they go forth from Jerusalem and proclaim *the word* everywhere.

LUKE

This *Commission* is to proclaim repentance into forgiveness of sins. This message is rooted in Christ's suffering and resurrection. We are called to admit that we both sin and receive that great gift of mercy. How else to say this?

The Ascension happens in Bethany, but then they return to Jerusalem to begin their *witnessing*. Note that the Greek word for *witness* is also the word for *martyr*.

But before witnessing they are to wait until they are *clothed out of the height with power*, which will come to be known as Pentecost.

In the temple they continue to be faithful Jews as well as disciples of Jesus. This kind of dual identity will become a challenge in the book of Acts, written by the same author as the gospel of Luke. In what way might you find yourself sometimes navigating two worlds?

As a scholar has put it, the only way out of the Gospel of Luke is through Jerusalem.

JOHN

Often referred to as *the Beloved Disciple*, the author of this fourth gospel, seems to want us to remember him as *the disciple whom Jesus loves*. That he had *leaned on* the *breast* of Jesus at the supper indeed suggests a relationship of intimacy.

Does Peter know there is some special way Jesus will look after the Beloved? Jesus cautions Peter to not worry about others, but *You follow me*; you just worry about your being my follower. In other words, mind your own disciple-ness.

The dialogue about the Beloved Disciple is an example of how people often hear something different from what we say or mean to say. It's hard to hear when I'm not listening.

In the last two verses, we are told these things have been written by the one referred through the gospel as *the disciple Jesus loves*.

Scholars think this is part of a second ending, added later, perhaps by friends of the author. Is it possible they also added the many references to *the disciple Jesus loves*?

There is a tradition that John, brother of James, son of Zebedee, spent a long life on the island of Patmos after taking care of Mary, the mother of Jesus, and that when people came to ask him to talk about Jesus he would simply say, *Little children, love one another*. What do you think of stories such as these?

The word *bibles* means libraries of books. What do you think of the *many other things* done by Jesus not written here?

Students in many parish schools perform different versions of the stations of the cross, and each of them has a particular flavor. One of them would bring it together with the Resurrection. Jesus has died and is carried into the tomb, and we wait. There is some music of expectancy and we wait. Music builds and we wait. Suddenly the eighth grade Jesus comes triumphantly out of the tomb as if he has just scored a touchdown, and everybody cheers with much joy. And relief.

FOR PONDERING

Leader Ponder in silence whether in these pages
something like one of these surfaced:

a seed planted,
> something I anticipate taking root and
> growing within me, and growing me…

a memory provoked,
> part of my story or our journey,
> whether pleasant or sad…

a question raised,
> something unknown
> to study, research, discuss with others,
> or further ponder…

an action prompted
> or a way to let God grow me into the
> human person God created me to be…

*Allow another minute for silent pondering,
and then the group may discuss the questions and ponderings
(restraining the urge to "fix" anybody).*

CLOSING PRAYER

When time is up

Leader Are there any intercessions to offer?

Leader Let us pray together the Easter Sequence:

All
Christians, to the Paschal Victim
   Offer your thankful praises!
A Lamb the sheep redeems;
   Christ, who only is sinless,
   Reconciles sinners to the Abba.
Death and life have contended
   in that combat stupendous:
   The Prince of life, who died,
   reigns eternal.
Speak, Mary, declaring
   What you saw, wayfaring.
   "The tomb of Christ, who is living,
      the glory of Jesus' resurrection;
      Bright angels attesting,
      the shroud and napkin resting;
      Yes, Christ my hope is arisen;
      To Galilee he goes before you."
Christ indeed from death is risen,
   our new life obtaining.
   Have mercy, victor Ruler, ever reigning!
   Amen. Alleluia.

Ye sons and daugh\-ters of the King,
With heav'n-ly hosts\ in glo\-ry sing,
To-day the grave\ has lost\ its sting:
                                      Al-le-lu-ia!

On that first morn\-ing of\ the week,
Be-fore the day\ be-gan\ to break,
The Ma-rys went\ their Lord\ to seek:
                                      Al-le-lu-ia!

An an-gel bade\ their sor\-row flee,
By speak-ing thus\ un-to\ the three:
"Your Lord is gone\ to Gal\-i-lee:"
                                      Al-le-lu-ia!

That night th'A-pos\-tles met\ in fear,
A-midst them came\ their Lord\ most dear
And said, "Peace be\ un-to\ you here:"
                                      Al-le-lu-ia!

Bless-ed are they\ that have\ not seen
And yet whose faith\ has con\-stant been,
In life e-ter\-nal they\ shall reign:
                                      Al-le-lu-ia!

And we with ho\-ly Church\ u-nite,
As ev-er-more\ is just\ and right,
In glo-ry to\ the King\ of light: Al-le-lu-ia!

Al-le-lu-ia\! Al-le\-lu-ia! Al-le-lu-ia!

> Text: see John 20; attributed to Jean Tisserand, d. 1494;
> translated by John M. Neal, 1851, altered
> Music: 888, O FILII ET FILIAE; Chant Mode II,
> *Airs sur les hymnes sacrez, odes et noels*, 1623

ALSO BY STEPHEN JOSEPH WOLF

The Resurrection in the Great Story of Jesus
**is the 11th short faith-sharing book
by former parish priest Stephen Joseph Wolf**
(ninety minutes once a week over six weeks)

1
PONDERING OUR FAITH

an introduction

1. The New Evangelization: revelation, faith, the trinity…
2. The Church: discipleship, community, family, prayer…
3. Sacraments: baptism, confirmation, eucharist, healing…
4. Vocation: holy orders, marriage, human dignity…
5. Moral Formation in Christ: grace, virtue, conscience…
6. The Sacred: liturgical year, art, music, devotions…

2
TREE of LIFE

Saint Bonaventure on the Christ Story
based on the Twelve Fruits of the *Tree of Life*.

The Mystery of the Incarnation
1. 1st Distinguished Origin; 2nd Humble Way of Life
2. 3rd Loft of his Power; 4th Plenitude of his Piety

The Mystery of his Passion
3. 5th Confidence in Trials; 6th Patience in Bad Treatment
4. 7th Constancy under Torture; 8th Victory in Conflict

The Mystery of his Glory
5. 9th The Novelty of his Resurrection; 10th Ascension
6. 11th Equity of his Judgment; 12th Eternal Kingdom

ALSO BY STEPHEN JOSEPH WOLF

3
FORTY PENANCES *for* SPIRITUAL EXERCISE
living the great gift of mercy

*These 40 "penances" are arranged following the Exercises of
St. Ignatius of Loyola to continue the conversion experience that
has already begun when one is aware that one has sinned.*

1. Reality of God's Complete Love
2. Reality of Sin and Reconciliation
3. Universal Call to Holiness   *seeds planted*
4. Vocation "Yes"   *memories provoked*
5. Perfect Act of Love   *questions raised*
6. Wholly New Way   *actions prompted*

4
THE PASSION
in the GREAT STORY of JESUS

*sets the four gospel narratives side-by-side
for prayer, reflection and conversation*

1. The Arrest
2. The Sanhedrin
3. Pilate
4. The Cross
5. The Death
6. The Burial

5
THE RESURRECTION
in the GREAT STORY of JESUS

*sets the four gospel narratives side-by-side
for prayer, reflection and conversation*

1. The Empty Tomb
2. Mary Magdalene
3. The Road to Emmaus
4. The Upper Room
5. The Seashore Breakfast
6. The Great Commission and the Ascension

ALSO BY STEPHEN JOSEPH WOLF

6
GOD's ONEs

a *so-what* book for the baptized

1. Baptized into Christ
2. Lifegiver Priest
3. Soldier Prophet
4. Footwasher Royal
5. Beloved Lover
6. Vocation Gifted (*Charisms*)

7
BEING SPOUSES

Unable to find a balanced parish resource about what marriage is, the author wrote this well-received work.

1. Marriage Sacramentality
2. The Domestic Church
3. Permanence
4. Fidelity
5. Children
6. Intimacy

8
GOD's MONEY

where faith meets life in the world

*Through 14 tax seasons,
the author became a certified public accountant and
an accredited personal financial specialist before entering seminary.
These chapters draw heavily from the experience of those years.*

1. Micah's Vine & Fig Tree
2. Daily Bread This Day
3. Building a Bigger Barn
4. Parables of Stewards
5. When Life is Changed
6. Community of Believers

***Everything
belongs to God.***
see Deut. 10:14

9
TWELVE-STEP SPIRITUALITY for CHRISTIANS

Following Vernon J. Bittner's *Twelve Steps for Christian Living*,
here is a helpful introduction to this very American spirituality
for those who may be unfamiliar with it.

1. When I Am Weak
2. Let Go and Let God
3. Sick As Our Secrets
4. Progress, Not Perfection   *because everyone*
5. Let It Begin With Me   *is addicted*
6. One Day At A Time   *to something*

10
ANGER the JESUS WAY

*reflections on the only gospel story where the author said Jesus
was angry, the healing of a man with a withered hand in Mark 3:1-6*

1. The Story
2. Watched in the Sabbath Assembly
3. Invited by Jesus
4. Riddle Silence   *Looking around at them*
5. Anger-Grief   *with anger, he grieved...*
6. Turning to Freedom   Mark 3:5

11
PLANNING MY OWN FUNERAL?

1. Vigil   *a four-week way to pray it*
2. Readings
3. Eucharist   *surprised we laughed*
4. Left Behind   *so much...*

www.ingramcontent.com/pod-product-compliance
Lightning Source LLC
Chambersburg PA
CBHW030200100526
44592CB00009B/368